CAN YOU SURVIVE
THE
BATTLE OF
RAGNARÖK?

An Interactive
Mythological Adventure

by Bruce Berglund

CAPSTONE PRESS
a capstone imprint

Published by Capstone Press, an imprint of Capstone
1710 Roe Crest Drive North Mankato, Minnesota 56003
capstonepub.com

Library of Congress Cataloging-in-Publication Data is available
on the Library of Congress website.
ISBN 9781666337808 (library binding)
ISBN 9781666337815 (paperback)
ISBN 9781666337822 (ebook PDF)

Summary: Ragnarök has come! It's the end of everything, including the reign of the
Norse gods. Odin, Thor, and the other gods will battle ancient enemies and giant
monsters to decide their destiny. As the fighting rages, the ground quakes and the
seas grow violent. Will you survive the final battle between the gods, giants, and
monstrous creatures of Norse mythology? Your choices will decide your fate. It's up
to YOU to decide how your story will unfold. Choose wisely!

Editorial Credits
Editor: Aaron Sautter; Designer: Bobbie Nuytten; Media Researcher: Morgan
Walters; Production Specialist: Polly Fisher

All internet sites appearing in back matter were available and accurate when this
book was sent to press.

Table of Contents

ABOUT YOUR ADVENTURE

Long ago, tales of the Norse gods were shared among peoples across much of northern Europe. Norse mythology describes a great battle, called Ragnarök, that will bring an end to everything. Will you fight the army of the dead or follow Odin to face his doom? Or perhaps you'll wield the great hammer Mjölnir in combat. Choose carefully. At Ragnarök, even the gods can be killed!

Chapter One sets the scene. Then you choose which path to take. Follow the directions at the bottom of each page. Your choices will determine what happens next. After you finish your path, go back and read the others for more adventures.

YOU CHOOSE the path you take through this mythical adventure.

In Norse mythology, Odin and the other gods watched over the worlds of the Norse cosmos from their home in Asgard.

Chapter 1
THE MIGHTY WINTER

Once upon a time, the Norse gods watched over the humans' world. Each day, Odin sent his two ravens, Huginn and Muninn, to watch over people and report back what they had seen. The noble Frey brought the sunshine and rain, so the crops would grow. The mighty Thor protected the humans from giants.

But Odin, Thor, and Frey are now asleep in Asgard. Most of the other gods sleep as well—except for Loki. His tricks went too far. He killed the great Baldur, son of Odin and brother of Thor. Now, Loki is imprisoned and being punished for his crimes. When there is an earthquake, it is Loki trying to break free.

Turn the page.

But there are few people left to be frightened by the earthquakes now. It is the time of Fimbulvetr—the Mighty Winter. For three years, there has been no warmth.

All of Midgard is dark and cold. The ground is frozen. Spring never comes, and the cruel wind comes from all directions. The cold has killed all the farm animals, and plows cannot cut through the frozen soil.

Across Midgard, people are starving. Family members are fighting each other for food. The few people left act like wild animals, searching empty towns for scraps of food.

The time of kings and queens is over. The time of great warriors who carried the axe and sword is past. People hide in the ruins of the great fortresses where royalty once lived.

Turn the page.

Most of the gods are warm in their beds.
But Heimdall, the watchman of the gods, stays
awake. He lives near the Rainbow Bridge that
connects Asgard and Midgard.

Heimdall can see far, even into the future.
Through the wind, he can hear a bird ruffle
its feathers to get warm. Close by, he keeps the
Gjallerhorn—the great horn that calls the gods.

Vidar, another son of Odin, is also awake.
He searches Midgard for pieces of leather from
old belts and shoes. He weaves the leather into
his boots. He must do this, but he does not
know why.

Vidar is near the sea when he sees a great
ship come out of the waves. The ship carries an
army of the wicked dead—warriors who lived
cruel lives and died shameful deaths. The army
is led by Loki, who's finally broken free from his
chains.

When a strong earthquake strikes, Heimdall looks in the distance and sees flames. It is Surt, the fire giant. He holds his burning sword and is leading warriors from Muspell, the realm of fire.

Vidar races to Heimdall. "It is time," says the son of Odin.

"Yes—it is time," says the guardian of the gods. Heimdall blows the Gjallerhorn.

Quickly, the gods awake from their sleep and put on their armor. Soon, they have gathered, ready for the final battle. What fate will you choose?

To fight the Midgard serpent as Thor, turn to page 13.

To go to battle as Heimdall, turn to page 37.

To face your fate as Vidar, turn to page 73.

Thor was believed to be the strongest and bravest of all the Norse gods.

Chapter 2

THOR VS. THE MIDGARD SERPENT

You are Odin's son, Thor—the god of thunder. The other gods all wear helmets, even your father. But not you. Your long hair blows in the cold wind.

When you heard the Gjallerhorn and rose from your bed, you put on a simple red tunic. You need no armor. But you put on the Power Belt, called Megingjord, that doubles your great strength.

You also wear the Jarngrieper, the Iron Gloves. They help you to wield your powerful hammer, Mjölnir, in battle.

Turn the page.

Mjölnir was made by the dwarves and is the mightiest of all the gods' weapons. Anything Mjölnir strikes is destroyed. If you throw the war hammer, you know it will hit the mark. And it will always fly back to your hand.

Your wife is Sif. She stands nearby with the other gods. She is beautiful. You are not. In fact, you have a rock stuck in your forehead from a fight with a giant.

Your daughter, Thrud, is one of the Valkyries. In the past, the Valkyries watched over the battles between humans. They chose which warriors would die and brought them to Valhalla, the great hall of the noble dead.

But now Thrud is here, ready to go to battle herself. Your sons are here as well. Their names are Modi and Magni—the Angry One and the Mighty One.

"This will be a mighty battle, my son," Odin says to you. "Surt the giant is coming. And Loki has broken free from his bonds."

"That's all?" you ask. "I've killed many giants. And you can handle Loki. Why did we need to wake everyone up?"

"Loki and Surt aren't alone," says Vidar. "Surt leads a large army of fiery warriors from Muspell. Loki has his own army as well. He's brought the wicked dead from the Underworld. Even more, the giant Hrym is with Loki, along with the frost giants. They're coming on a giant ship, the largest I have ever seen."

"There are still more enemies coming," says Heimdall. "I see Fenrir the giant wolf. He has broken his chains and is coming from the mountains. Fire shoots from his nostrils, and he devours everything in his path."

Turn the page.

Heimdall turns toward the sea and looks into the distance. "I also see the serpent Jormungand. He has risen from the deep and is coming to shore."

"The wolf and serpent are children of Loki," says Odin. "They have come to bring vengeance on us, for casting Loki into the Underworld."

Odin turns to you. "You are the strongest and bravest of us all," he says. "Where will you fight?"

"I know how to kill giants," you say. You point to the rock stuck in your forehead. "I have this from when I killed Hrugnir, the mightiest of giants." Hrugnir hurled a stone at you just as you threw Mjölnir. The hammer killed the giant, but a piece of the rock stuck in your head.

"But I have hunted the serpent a long time," you add.

To fight the fiery giant Surt, go to page 17.
To battle Jormungand the serpent, turn to page 22.

The gods set off in different directions to face their enemies. You will stay to guard the Rainbow Bridge.

"Father, we shall stand with you," says Magni. His brother Modi nods.

"Thank you, my sons," you answer. "You stood with me against Hrugnir. You are both great in strength and courage."

You remember your battle against Hrugnir. After your hammer smashed the giant, he fell on top of you. His enormous leg pinned you to the ground. Thankfully, Magni and Modi were there to lift the giant's leg and set you free.

"But I have never faced this giant," you say, pointing to Surt. "I do not know his strength."

Surt is larger than any giant you have faced. And you can see heat rising from his body like a burning coal.

Turn the page.

Fire flows from the sword in Surt's hand. When he swings the blade, a wave of fire melts the snow and scorches the ground. His army marches over blackened ground. When Surt stops, you can smell him. He reeks of smoke and sulfur.

You stand with Magni and Modi before the Rainbow Bridge. "You know me, giant!" you shout. "I am Thor, god of thunder, killer of giants."

The giant lowers his flaming sword and points it at you. A bolt of fire bursts from the sword and scorches the ends of your beard.

Surt's bolt of fire surges past you and engulfs the Rainbow Bridge. Magni and Modi rush to the bridge, but the fire is too hot. They stop and cover their faces. Although the bridge is made of light and color, it burns like dry wood.

Myths say that the giant Surt will lead an army of warriors from his fiery world of Muspell to battle the gods at Ragnarök.

"I am Surt," the giant calls. "My home is the volcano at the edge of Muspell, the realm of fire."

"These are sons of Muspell," he says gesturing toward his army. The warriors are also giants, glowing with heat. "We come to bring destruction to all of Midgard."

Turn the page.

Surt points his sword toward the plain of Vigrid. His army turns and begins to march. They are ready to face the gods in battle.

"Look, father!" says Modi. He points to the cliffs at the edge of the plain. You see the serpent Jormungand gliding over the cliff wall.

You turn to look back at Surt, but the giant is swinging his flaming sword at you!

To avoid Surt's attack and fight the serpent instead, go to page 21.

To stay and battle Surt, turn to page 26.

At the last moment, you duck. Surt's flaming sword narrowly misses your head.

"Stay and fight the giant!" you shout to Magni and Modi.

You leap into your chariot and dash toward the seashore. In the distance, you see the ocean churning like a boiling pot. Giant waves of black and gray water crash against the shore. As you get closer, the salty spray freezes on your beard and stings your eyes.

You see the great Njord, god of the sea, standing in the waves. The waves smash into his chest and shoulders. He holds his spear above the water.

You squint your eyes to see through the wind and spray. Further out to sea, a dark shape rises from the water. The serpent Jormungand uncoils. It looms over the god like a fortress tower.

Turn to page 24.

Your chariot is pulled by two strong goats, Snarler and Grinder. They bring you swiftly to the seashore, to a place called Noatun—Place of the Boats. People once fished there, but the winter winds have smashed their boats and docks to splinters.

You once went to sea to catch Jormungand, but the serpent escaped from you. The giant beast has been your enemy for ages.

As you reach the shore, you see the serpent for the first time. Jormungand's fangs are as long as tree trunks and as sharp as swords. On both sides of the creature's neck, enormous sacs of venom swell out.

The giant serpent snaps its head forward like a whip, and venom sprays from its fangs. The deadly poison kills whatever it touches. Sea birds fall from the sky. Dead fish bubble up from the depths.

Jormungand, or the Midgard Serpent, was thought to be so huge that it could stretch around the entire world.

Turn the page.

Njord, the god of the sea, stands in the pounding waves, ready to meet Jormungand. Njord reaches back to throw his spear.

Yet the serpent is too quick. Its tail lashes, and a huge wave smashes into Njord. The god disappears under the water. Jormungand then sprays venom over the waves.

"Njord!" you shout. But even the voice of mighty Thor cannot be heard through the roaring wind.

The waves are thick with dead creatures, killed by the serpent's venom. But there is no sign of Njord. Jormungand plunges into the water and starts swimming toward shore. You stand on the rocks, holding Mjölnir.

"My hammer does not miss its target," you say to yourself. "But Njord was god of the sea, and he could not defeat the serpent."

Njord was the Norse god of the wind and the sea. He was said to control the fates of sailors and fishermen.

You look back. Behind you the cliffs rise from the sea to the plain. What would be the best way to fight the beast?

To fight Jormungand
from high ground, turn to page 27.

To fight the serpent
at the shore, turn to page 32.

You call out to your sons. "Stop the army! I will face Surt myself."

Magni and Modi charge into the legion of giants. Like you, they are strong and brave. Together, they cut down the warriors of Muspell like timber.

"Your army will be defeated!" you shout to Surt. "And you will fall as well."

You pull back Mjölnir, ready to throw the great hammer. But then Surt sweeps his sword before him. Fire rushes from the blade like a river of lava. You lift an arm to protect yourself. Your iron gloves glow red hot from the fire, but they can't protect you for long. You roar in pain as the flames swallow you. Hopefully Magni and Modi survive the battle longer than you did.

THE END
To follow another path, turn to page 11.
To learn more about Ragnarök, turn to page 101.

You turn away from the waves and climb the rocky cliffs. The wind batters you on the narrow path. As you reach the top, you look below. Jormungand is at the shore. The serpent scoops dead sea creatures into its gaping jaws. Its tail thrashes the docks and boats into splinters.

The plain of Vigrid stretches before you. You see the legion of gods, ready for battle. Enemies surround them. On one side is Loki's army of frost giants and the wicked dead. On the other side, the giants of Muspell stand ready to fight.

You spy a rocky mound near you. *That is where I'll make my stand against the serpent*, you think. As you take your ground, you hear the voices of your sons.

"Father!" calls Modi, rushing toward you. "We cannot stand against Surt's fiery sword. It burns everything in his path."

Turn the page.

"I must defeat the serpent," you say to your sons. "He has killed the god of the sea. Stand with me."

Just then, you hear the sound of Jormungand's scales scraping over the cliff's edge. The serpent lifts its enormous body. You throw Mjölnir toward the creature's head, but the serpent is too quick. The hammer misses its target and flies back to your hand.

"You have never missed before," you say, looking curiously at the hammer of the gods.

You hurl the hammer again, aiming for the serpent's belly. Mjölnir hits the beast, but does not break through its hide. The beast's scales are like the thickest, hardest iron armor. The hammer flies back to your hand.

"Father!" calls Magni. "Here is my axe!"

Thor and Jormungand were mortal enemies in several Norse myths.

Magni the Strong holds out his great battle axe. No other god can swing its heavy blade— except for you.

To fight with Magni's axe, turn to page 30.

To keep fighting with Mjölnir, turn to page 34.

"Throw it to me!" you shout to Magni.

Magni heaves the battle axe to you. You catch its thick wooden handle. You now have two weapons—the battle axe in your left hand and Mjölnir in your right.

With the speed of a whip, you hurl Mjölnir toward Jormungand's head. This time it finds its mark. The hammer smashes into the serpent's jaw. Jormungand is stunned.

You then leap forward, and with a mighty swing, you plunge the great battle axe into the monster's throat.

You feel the sharp iron slice through flesh and bone. Jormungand lets out a gruesome shriek as its head separates from its body.

Mjölnir returns to your hand as you watch the serpent's head twist through the sky. You smile at the defeat of the wretched beast.

But then Jormungand's head crashes to the ground like a giant boulder. The impact cracks the beast's skull like a shattered pot. Broken pieces of bone pierce the serpent's huge venom sacs. The poisonous oil sprays out, covering you from head to toe.

You are the god of thunder. But the monster's venom is too powerful even for you. You scream in pain and die.

THE END

To follow another path, turn to page 11.
To learn more about Ragnarök, turn to page 101.

"Njord!" you call out again. But there is no sign of the god of the sea.

The waves push dead fish, birds, and sea creatures onto the shore. Jormungand is getting closer. Its jaws are open wide, showing its enormous fangs. You pull back your hammer and prepare to throw it.

"Jormungand!" you shout. "I have hunted you for ages. Today will be our last fight!"

The serpent rears back its head, and its venom sacs billow out. Just as you swing your arm to throw Mjölnir, the beast sprays its oily, poisonous venom all over you.

At first, you seem fine. "Ha! Is that the best you can do?" you scoff.

But the poison works quickly. In moments, pain courses through your body. Soon you feel your strength fade, and you drop to your knees.

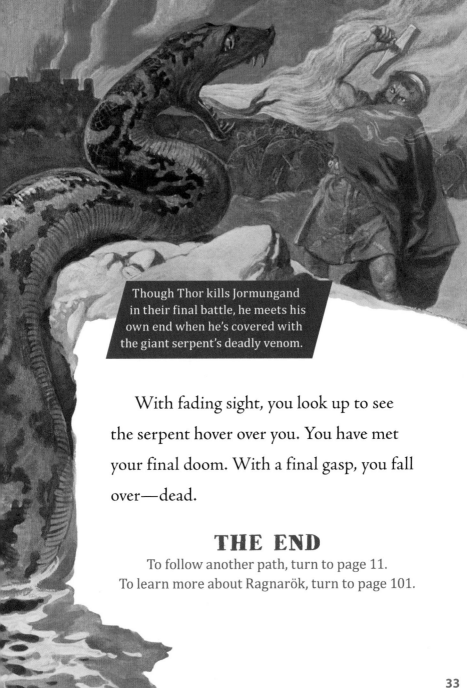

Though Thor kills Jormungand in their final battle, he meets his own end when he's covered with the giant serpent's deadly venom.

With fading sight, you look up to see the serpent hover over you. You have met your final doom. With a final gasp, you fall over—dead.

THE END

To follow another path, turn to page 11.
To learn more about Ragnarök, turn to page 101.

"Keep your axe!" you shout to Magni.

You lift Mjölnir high above your head and smash it down onto the rock. A wall of thunder bursts from the hammer and crashes into the serpent. The great beast is stunned. It shakes its head like a dog, trying to gain its senses.

You thrust Mjölnir at the serpent and blast a bolt of lightning into Jormungand's belly. The serpent shrieks in pain. A smoking black wound opens in its scales. The monster sways back and forth, dazed from its injuries.

You decide to throw the great hammer again. This time Mjölnir finds its target, smashing Jormungand between the eyes.

As the hammer returns to your hand, you watch Jormungand's body lose its strength. The serpent's massive body falls slowly to the ground like a mighty tree.

But the serpent is not dead, only stunned.
It slowly lifts its eyelids to look at you and then
breathes out a cruel, raspy hiss.

With your boot, you press Jormungand's
neck to the ground and lift the hammer over
your head. It's time to finish the evil creature.
You swing Mjölnir into Jormungand's skull. The
bones crumble under the hammer's great force.

But shards of the serpent's skull pierce its
venom sacs. The black poison bursts forth and
splatters all over you.

Although you are the strongest of the gods,
the serpent's poison is stronger. You fall over and
take your last breath.

THE END

To follow another path, turn to page 11.
To learn more about Ragnarök, turn to page 101.

In Norse myths, Heimdall called the gods to battle with the Gjallerhorn. The long, magical horn could be heard across the Norse cosmos.

Chapter 3

HEIMDALL THE BOLD WATCHER

You are Heimdall, the watcher. More than other gods, you shine with a golden brightness. Even your teeth are golden. As the watcher, you have seen armies moving to battle. You have called the gods to gather at the Rainbow Bridge.

"This is the great battle," says Odin. "Surt the giant is coming with his flaming sword. And Loki has broken free from his bonds."

"Loki and Surt are not alone," you say. "Surt leads an army—the evil warriors of Muspell, the realm of fire. Loki has an army too. He has brought the wicked dead from the Underworld. The giant Hrym travels with Loki as well, along with all the frost giants."

Turn the page.

"There are even more enemies," you continue, pointing toward the mountains. "Fenrir the giant wolf has broken his chains. Fire shoots from his nostrils, and he devours everything in his path."

You turn toward the sea and look into the distance. "I can also see the serpent Jormungand. He has risen from the deep and is coming to shore."

"The wolf and the serpent are children of Loki," says Odin. "They have come to bring vengeance on us for casting Loki into the Underworld."

The gods decide which enemies they will face.

"I will face Jormungand," says Thor.

"I will meet the wolf Fenrir," says Odin.

Frey, the noble god, sets off to meet Surt the giant. The other gods will march to the plain of Vigrid to battle the warriors of Muspell and Loki's army.

Will you stay here and keep watch at your post or go to watch over the coming battle?

To stay and watch what unfolds, turn to page 40.

To join in the fight, turn to page 45.

Your place is here at the Rainbow Bridge between Asgard and Midgard. For ages, you have watched over the realm of humans. You reported their doings to the gods. Now you watch the gods set off in different directions as their strong, fearsome enemies approach in the distance.

You fear this day will not be like the days of old. You remember how you helped Thor win back his hammer from the ogres ages ago. Thor killed many enemies that day.

As you keep watch, you see Thor kill his enemy. You see the god of thunder smash Jormungand's head with his hammer. You watch Thor stand back as the serpent falls to the ground.

But his victory is not like the others. You watch the evil serpent spray venom over Thor with its dying breath. The mighty god cries out in pain and falls to the ground. Thor is dead.

You turn and look to the mountains. There you see Odin stand against Fenrir the great wolf. Odin plunges his spear into the wolf's mouth, but Fenrir's fangs snap the spear in half.

The wolf then lunges and grabs Odin in its jaws. Fenrir crushes the god with its teeth and swallows him down. Odin, the wise king of the gods, the All-father, is gone.

You then look to Frey, the noble god. Frey stands against Surt the giant. The giant sweeps his flaming sword, and a wave of fire burns everything before him. Frey is swallowed by the flames.

On the plain of Vigrid, you see the last of the gods fight against the giants of Muspell. Beyond them, Loki's army has climbed up onto the cliffs from the sea. Enemies approach from all sides. The gods will soon be overwhelmed.

Turn the page.

At Ragnarök, most of the Norse gods will meet their end as they battle their enemies on the plain of Vigrid.

You take up your sword, the fierce blade called Hofund. Now is not the time for watching. It is time to enter the battle!

To fight the giant Surt, go to page 43.

To go to battle against Loki's army, turn to page 45.

To face Fenrir the giant wolf, turn to page 46.

You don't have to go far to meet the giant. With heavy steps, Surt approaches the Rainbow Bridge that connects Asgard and Midgard. You hold up your sword to block his way.

"Step aside," the giant growls.

"I am the guardian of this bridge," you declare. "You will not touch it. It has stood for ages. It will always connect the realm of the gods and the world of humans."

The giant laughs. "You fool," he says. "Today will see the end of both gods and humans."

The giant lowers his huge flaming sword. A bolt of fire bursts past you and engulfs the Rainbow Bridge.

The Rainbow Bridge always burned with its own light and color. But now it bursts into flames like dry firewood. You try to reach it, but the heat is too strong.

Turn the page.

You turn back to Surt. The giant lifts his flaming sword above his head.

"The realm of fire will sweep you all away," Surt says in his deep rumbling voice. "Today is the end of the gods."

The giant swings his sword down, and a river of fire flows from the blade. The flames race toward you like a wave. You try to block the fire with your arms. But today you have met your fate.

THE END

To follow another path, turn to page 11.
To learn more about Ragnarök, turn to page 101.

Your horse carries you quickly across the battlefield of Vigrid to the cliff's edge, where the flat, snowy land drops to the sea. Down below, Loki's great ship has reached the shore. You have never seen such a large ship. It is filled with the wicked dead and frost giants.

There is a narrow path up the side of the cliff, wide enough only for Loki's troops to march single file. Loki sends the frost giants up first. But their wide feet are too large for the path. They struggle to keep balance as they climb.

You look back. Behind you is a rocky ledge rising above the snow-covered plain. Should you meet Loki's forces head on or try to pick a better position?

To climb down the path to face Loki's army, turn to page 48.

To climb up the ledge to higher ground, turn to page 51.

You reach the edge of the mountain forest, where the plain begins. The great wolf pushes his way through the trees. The ragged fur of his back reaches the treetops. The pines fall like matchsticks.

The giant wolf Fenrir was said to have jaws so wide that they could stretch from the ground to the sky.

Fenrir stands on the plain. The beast lowers his head to look straight at you. His fangs are like iron spikes. With each breath, fire comes from his nostrils.

You lift the sword Hofund before you. But the wolf is too quick. Fenrir snaps you up in his jaws before you can react. You roar in pain as the fangs close around you. You are still able to swing Hofund. The blade cuts Fenrir's snout, but the wolf does not feel the pain.

Fenrir swings his head back and swallows you into the black.

THE END

To follow another path, turn to page 11.
To learn more about Ragnarök, turn to page 101.

You move quickly down the path, holding your sword Hofund ready to strike.

The first giant to come up the path doesn't see you. He's busy watching his feet as he climbs the narrow path. You swing your sword, and Hofund slices through him. The giant's skin is like ice. It cracks and shatters. He falls off the cliff to the sea below. You then cut down another frost giant, then another, and another.

But the eighth giant is ready and waiting for you. He swings an axe across the path. You duck, and the blade smashes into the cliff wall.

"Do not stop!" calls a voice from below. It is Hrym, the giants' leader. "Push forward!"

The giants lower their shoulders and surge forward. You slash at the head of the line. Hofund cuts through the lead giant's legs, and he falls from the path.

But the next giant is already pushing you back, raising a spear above his head. You thrust your sword into his icy belly. Another giant pushes forward, swinging an axe. Then another swings at you with a sword.

There are too many. You turn and dash up the path as the giants rush after you. You risk pausing to look back. The giants are moving quickly. Some stumble off the path, but the ones behind continue to push forward.

"Move!" Hrym yells. "Get to the top!"

You look down the cliff and see the full size of Loki's army. More frost giants, followed by hundreds of dead soldiers, are all marching single file up the path.

Before you can react, another giant is upon you. He's lifting an axe high over his head to bring it down onto yours.

Turn the page.

But before he can strike, you plunge Hofund into his ribs. It's like thrusting a sword into ice-covered water. He falls, but the next giant is already there.

You turn to run up the path to the high ground. But you're stopped in your tracks. A frost giant grabs you. His icy fingers crush your arms and ribs. The giant throws you off the path, and you see Loki laughing as you plunge to your death. The raging sea will be your grave.

THE END

To follow another path, turn to page 11.
To learn more about Ragnarök, turn to page 101.

You reach the rocky ledge rising above the flat plain. It is as high as a giant's shoulders. It's an ideal place to stand against Loki's army.

The first giants climb over the cliff's edge. When they see you they rush across the snowy plain. The giants swing their swords and axes, but they cannot reach you up on the ledge. You cut them down easily with Hofund.

The next giants do not rush toward you. One by one, they climb over the cliff edge and form a line to prepare for battle.

But their actions are strange. You know that giants don't fight in lines, especially frost giants. They're not very bright. They normally rely on size and strength rather than strategy.

However, these giants are being directed by Hrym. He shouts orders to them as they climb over the cliff's edge.

Turn the page.

At Ragnarök, Loki will lead an army of the wicked dead from the Underworld into battle. These warriors led cruel and hateful lives in the land of the living.

Behind Hrym come the wicked dead. For ages, they've been punished for their wrongs in the depths of the Underworld. Their skin is rotten and falls off their bodies, showing the bones underneath.

The wicked dead line up away from the frost giants. They were once warriors, so they know how to follow orders. There are hundreds of dead soldiers. They move slowly, dragging their feet in the snow. They don't speak or make any sound. You hear only their rusty swords and spears clattering as they form their ranks.

After the ranks of the wicked dead have taken their place, Loki himself climbs over the edge of the cliff. He's been bound in chains for years, but Loki looks the same. He is still handsome, with mischievous eyes and a twisted, wicked smile. He carries Laevateinn, the magic spear that changes shape—and never misses its target.

Turn the page.

Loki sees you and laughs. "The gods sent their watchman to face me?" he asks. "Did you not see this army from your post, watchman? Did you not warn the other gods?"

You do not answer Loki's taunts. He laughs again. He is no warrior. He's a trickster. He disguises himself to fool others. And now he's pretending to be a general.

Loki shouts orders to his army and points. Hrym and the frost giants begin to move away from the cliff's edge to your left. Loki then points in the other direction. The evil dead from the Underworld move from the cliff's edge to your right.

"You must choose, watchman! Who will you fight?" Loki calls.

To fight the giants, go to page 55.
To fight the wicked dead, turn to page 60.

You leap from the rocky ledge into the line of frost giants. They are large and strong, but you are quick, and Hofund is a swift, sharp blade. The sword easily cuts through the giants' icy skin.

The frost giants are crowded together. You quickly dash around and behind them. One swings his sword at you and misses. His blade cuts into another giant, who topples into a third. Another lifts his axe over his head to chop you down. But he reaches too far back, and the blade hits another giant's head. That one punches out in anger and hits a different giant.

You duck and dodge among the giants. You stab your sword into giant legs and giant bellies. The sharp blade cracks open their icy skin.

You do not kill even half of the giants. But they quickly grow angry and begin fighting each other with their own swords, spears, axes, and fists. They do not even try to find you.

Turn the page.

You step away from the mob of giants and watch as they brawl in the snow. Hrym also stands away from the mob.

"Stop!" he shouts. "Stop!" But the giants do not hear their leader. They growl in anger and roar in pain.

Then you hear another roar. You turn to see another army thundering across the plain of Vigrid. These warriors charge toward Loki's troops of the dead.

You know this army. It is the Einherjar— the Army of One. These warriors are the noble dead. They were great heroes and kings, famous for their bravery, honor, and loyalty. After their deaths, they were brought to Valhalla by the Valkyries. In the great hall at Asgard, they feasted with Odin. Now they storm the plain of Vigrid with the Valkyries.

With Loki's army busy with the Einherjar, you turn back to the giants. The last two swing their weapons at each other and strike a mortal blow. They drop to the ground at the same moment, atop a great mound of dead giants.

The only one left standing is Hrym. He looks in disgust at his dead troops. Then he looks up at you. His face twists in anger. He lets out a fierce shout and charges. Hrym lifts his axe over his head and prepares to swing.

You race forward to meet him. But just as Hrym draws close enough to bring down his axe, you roll to the ground. As one of his massive feet passes over you, you slice it off with your sword. You jump to your feet and watch the giant fall.

Blood from the giant's wound soaks the snow. Hrym tries to push himself up, using the axe handle as a crutch. But he cannot lift his great weight. He looks back at you.

Turn the page.

"You may have won this battle," he growls. "But you will lose the war. Today will bring the end of the gods. You are the watchman. You can see that."

You plunge Hofund into Hrym's neck, and the giant lets out his last gurgling breath.

The giant Hrym will lead the frost giants from Jotunheim into battle at Ragnarök.

But suddenly, a terrible pain shoots through your body. You look down. The point of Loki's spear is sticking out of your chest. Slowly, you turn around to see Loki standing among the bodies of his troops and the Einherjar. They are all slain. He alone survives.

You collapse to your knees as Loki walks toward you. Your vision is getting blurry, but you can see Loki smirking.

"Today, I have my vengeance," he says. "All of the gods have met their final destiny."

You fall on your side in the snow. Your eyes close. No more will you be the watcher of the gods.

THE END
To follow another path, turn to page 11.
To learn more about Ragnarök, turn to page 101.

You take a step toward Loki's army, then stop. With your keen ears, you hear a distant, rumbling sound. With your sharp eyes, you look back.

Then you see them, the Einherjar—the Army of One. The troops are the noble dead, great heroes and kings, famous for their bravery, honor, and loyalty. After their deaths, they were brought to Valhalla by the Valkyries. In the great hall at Asgard, they feasted with Odin. But they prepared every day, ready to go to battle once again.

You step off the rocky ledge onto the snowy plain. You walk calmly toward Loki's army. Your arms are open, inviting the troops to attack. The wicked dead look at you with confusion.

"What are you waiting for?" shouts Loki. "Charge!"

The troops look at Loki, and they look at you. They walk forward to meet you. You urge them to come. You look back to the frost giants too. They're also confused by what you're doing.

As you listen, you can hear the noise growing louder. Suddenly, you let out a shout and charge. Many of the wicked dead were cowards in their past lives. Even though you are just one fighter, they turn and run.

But others charge at you. They let out their own growls. The noise covers the sound of thundering feet and hooves. Loki's troops are getting closer and closer to you. But they can't hear what's coming until it's too late.

Behind you, the Einherjar leap over the rocky ledge. The great heroes and kings smash into Loki's army. The Valkyrie veer off on their horses and attack the frost giants.

Turn the page.

You follow the Einherjar into battle. Hofund cuts through the shameful dead. Yet Loki's army fights back savagely. The Einherjar suffer terrible losses. The lifeless bodies of both the wicked and noble fall to the snow-covered ground.

You look up and see that the Valkyries are also falling, even as they defeat the frost giants. No one will survive this battle.

Soon you notice a figure moving among the Einherjar. He wears the robes of an ancient king, one of the Einherjar himself. But as you watch, he approaches one of the noble warriors from behind and strikes him down. With your sharp eyes, you can see what no one else can. This is no king. It's Loki in disguise!

As you slay the last of Loki's troops, Loki himself cuts down the last of the Einherjar.

"Loki!" you shout. He returns to his own appearance, handsome and devious. Around you are the lifeless bodies of the Einherjar and Loki's troops. You see that the frost giants and Valkyries have cut each other down. No one else is left standing on the battlefield.

To your left, between you and Loki, is a rocky ledge. Can you reach it first and take the high ground? Or should you charge straight at Loki?

To run for the rocky ledge, turn to page 64.
To attack Loki head on, turn to page 68.

You and Loki move at the same time. You both race for the rocky ledge. Loki is thin and light, while Hofund is heavy in your hand. He reaches the ledge just before you and leaps on top. Loki swings his sword down and slices your left shoulder.

You step back and swing at Loki's feet. The god of mischief jumps to avoid your blade. He swings down again, cutting open your other shoulder.

Heimdall and Loki will each meet their fate during their final battle at the end of the world.

You stagger backward. The pain is fierce. You try to lift Hofund with both hands, but the strength in your arms is fading. You drop to your knees. Loki jumps down from the ledge.

"Heimdall the watcher," says Loki. "The god who sees far into the distance. Did you not know this is the day of Ragnarök—the final destiny of the gods?

"Look around," Loki continues mockingly. "Where is Thor? Where is Odin? They are all gone. It's the end of gods and the end of those worthless humans."

Loki thrusts his sword into your ribs. You gasp in pain. Then Loki puts a boot against your chest to pull his sword from your body.

You fall to the ground and lie in the snow. You feel your life draining away. Your hand still grasps Hofund.

Turn the page.

You hear the snow crunch under Loki's boots. The wily god lowers himself down to look you in the eye.

"It's finished," Loki says. "I won."

But as he mocks you, Loki doesn't see your arm tense with new strength. You swing Hofund, and the blade cuts through Loki's armor, slicing him open. He falls back, and his blood pours out onto the snow.

You have enough strength to lift yourself up and look at Loki. "I see further than you," you tell him. "Yes, today is the end of Odin and Thor. But other gods will live. And there are humans who will live.

"Today is the end of Loki," you say. "You will never be victorious. I have seen that. There will be new life out of this death. Today sees the beginning of a new age."

You watch Loki's eyes as he looks into the sky. Snowflakes land on his eyelashes. But he does not blink. He breathes no more. Loki, the trickster god, lies lifeless on the plain of Vigrid, still and cold.

You lie back to rest. Soon you hear the growing roar of a great fire from Surt's sword. You feel the heat, and the snow beneath you melts. You close your eyes for the last time and welcome your fate.

THE END

To follow another path, turn to page 11.
To learn more about Ragnarök, turn to page 101.

You walk toward Loki. The blood-stained snow is covered with lifeless bodies.

Loki walks toward you as well.

"You sounded the horn too late!" he shouts at you. "You were watchman of the gods, and you did not see what was coming. You had one job, and you failed."

You keep walking without speaking.

"Nothing to say?" Loki calls. "Perhaps you were asleep at your post. You missed the signs. The gods are dead! They've paid the price for locking me away."

You are tired of Loki's taunts. You charge toward him and strike hard with Hofund. But Loki's armor is strong, and the blow glances off. He swings his sword, but you block it. The sound of clashing blades rings across the plain of Vigrid.

The fight is fierce. You slash, and Loki slashes back. He stabs, and you defend yourself. Eventually you rip through each other's armor, cutting deep wounds. Loki staggers with pain. His handsome face is streaked with blood. You can barely lift Hofund. Its weight is too much for your slashed arms.

"Time to finish this," says Loki. With the last of his strength, he charges forward with his sword. You have a last measure of strength as well. You lift Hofund to meet Loki's charge. The two swords plunge in deep—yours into Loki's body and his into you. Your faces are close. Your eyes narrow, and you each twist your blade. You and Loki fall to the snow. Each of you looks up to the dark gray sky.

"My vengeance is finally complete," Loki says. "You are the last of the gods. You will die, and I will win."

Turn the page.

"No," you say simply. "You are wrong. My sight reaches farther than yours. I am not the last of the gods. I can see the son of Odin and the sons of Thor."

You turn your head to see Loki's pale face. "This is not the end. You have failed."

For once, Loki has nothing to say. No more tricks, no more taunts, no more lies. He is silent.

As Loki dies, you see the flames from Surt's giant sword. The fire spreads across the battlefield, burning everything in sight.

You can see what will come. There will be a new age of gods and humans. You lie back and close your eyes. The fire will wipe away the old age, so a new age can begin.

THE END

To follow another path, turn to page 11.
To learn more about Ragnarök, turn to page 101.

Vidar (left) was one of Odin's many sons. His mother was a giantess named Grid.

Chapter 4
VIDAR'S DEADLY JOURNEY

You are Vidar, one of Odin's sons. The other gods look to your father. The king of the gods is wearing a golden helmet and chain mail armor. He carries the powerful spear Gungnir that was made for him ages ago by the dwarves. He is ready for battle.

The gods wait for his orders. But he gives none. "I must go to Yggdrasil, the World Tree," he says.

You're surprised, as are the other gods. "We need you to join us in battle," says the noble Frey.

"I will join soon enough," says Odin. "But I must first seek wisdom, even greater wisdom than I possess."

Turn the page.

Odin mounts Sleipnir, his magical eight-legged horse, and races in the direction of Yggdrasil. Thor, the god of thunder, rides his chariot to the sea to battle the giant serpent Jormungand. Heimdall the watcher sets off to the cliffs to face Loki and his army.

Meanwhile, the other gods, including Hermod, Tyr, and Ull, all march to the plain of Vigrid to meet their enemies in battle. In the distance you see the giant Surt, holding his flaming sword and marching with his fiery army.

Will you follow your father or choose to face Surt in battle?

To follow Odin to Yggdrasil, go to page 75.
To fight against the giant Surt, turn to page 78.

Sleipnir is a swift horse. His many legs carry Odin quickly to Yggdrasil. Your own horse races to keep up.

Yggdrasil is an enormous ash tree. It stands at the center of the world. Its roots stretch to each of the nine worlds. The tree's trunk is as thick as hundreds of giants. Its branches reach to the heavens and spread far in every direction. The leaves and trunk are sprinkled with sacred white mud.

Near Yggdrasil's trunk is a deep well. It plunges down past the roots. At the bottom is the head of Mimir, a god who lived ages ago. Mimir was great in wisdom, even greater than Odin. But some gods were jealous of his wisdom and killed him. Odin put Mimir's head in the deep well. At times, Odin goes to the well to ask Mimir for advice.

Turn the page.

You follow your father down to the well and watch as he leans over it. He speaks and then listens. He closes his eyes and nods. Then he stands up and faces you.

"What did you learn, father?" you ask.

"I have learned what will happen this day," answers Odin. "And what will happen after. Come, there is much to do, my son."

Standing before Yggdrasil, Odin holds out his arms and calls out. "Come forth, my guests! Come from your feast at Valhalla. This is the day you have prepared for!"

At the sound of Odin's voice, the leaves of Yggdrasil rustle. From its branches appear the Einherjar—the noble dead. They are the great heroes and kings who died in battle ages ago.

After their deaths, these noble warriors were brought to Valhalla, the great hall at Asgard. Every day, they feasted with Odin. And every day, they prepared for battle—this battle.

The Einherjar ride off to the plain of Vigrid. They will face Loki's army of evil dead and frost giants.

"Are you riding with the Einherjar, father?" you ask.

"No," answers Odin. "My fate lies with another enemy—the great wolf Fenrir. You can ride with me or follow the Einherjar into battle."

To ride into battle with the noble dead, turn to page 81.

To ride with Odin and face the mighty wolf, turn to page 84.

You watch Odin ride off on Sleipnir. Then, one of the other gods speaks.

"Join me," says the noble god Frey. "We will face the giant Surt and his army together."

You and Frey race to meet Surt at the Rainbow Bridge. The giant and his warriors are already there, crossing over from Muspell, the realm of fire. You see heat rising from Surt's hulking body. Fire flows from the long sword in his hand. His soldiers glow like burning coals. You can smell them. They reek of smoke and ash.

Ages ago, the gods built the Rainbow Bridge to connect their world to the realm of humans. The bridge is made of colorful light and glimmers like the stars. But now the bridge shakes under the weight of Surt's army. You see the bridge collapsing behind the line of warriors. The rainbow colors disappear, and the bridge breaks apart and burns like dry sticks.

Norse myths stated that the Bifrost, or Rainbow Bridge, connected Asgard to Midgard, or Earth, the world of humans.

Frey moves to the foot of the bridge. The noble god once carried a magic sword that could fight on its own, without a hand to hold it. But Frey lost the sword ages ago. Now he carries a deer's antler as his weapon. He has killed giants before with the antler.

Turn the page.

"You have no sword," says Surt. "Even if you did, you would not stop me."

Surt swings his flaming sword. Fire rushes from its blade like a river, and the flames pour over Frey like a waterfall.

The fire flows toward you. You crouch behind your shield for protection. But the heat is too great. The shield melts like candle wax, and you cry out in pain as the fire swallows you.

THE END

To follow another path, turn to page 11.
To learn more about Ragnarök, turn to page 101.

You ride alongside the Einherjar. The army includes great kings who once ruled over the lands of Midgard. Some are great heroes who won fame for their bravery and loyalty. Even though they died years ago, their robes and armor are like new.

In the distance you see Loki's army. His troops look much different. They are the wicked dead, warriors who acted with cruelty, hate, and injustice during their lives. Their robes are tattered, and their skin is rotten.

As you gallop across the snowy plain of Vigrid, you see that Heimdall is already fighting Loki's troops. The watcher has no fear, and his sword slays many of the wicked dead. But Heimdall does not see the frost giants approaching from another direction. Led by the fierce Hrym, they are moving to join the fight. You must stop them.

Turn the page.

You steer your horse away from the Einherjar toward the giants. You charge straight into the pack of giants, swinging your sword to the left and right. The giants' skin breaks apart like ice as they fall under your sword.

The giants are surprised by your attack and swing their weapons wildly. But your horse is smart and quick. You weave between the slow giants and continue to strike them down.

Suddenly, you are knocked off your horse, as if you rode into a large tree branch. But it's not a tree branch—it's Hrym's enormous arm!

You are stunned and dizzy. "Where is my sword?" you ask in a groggy voice. You see it lying in the snow, close by. You try to reach for it, but suddenly your hand disappears! Hrym's axe has cut off your arm at the elbow.

"Aauggh!" you cry out in pain.

You roll on your back, holding what's left of your bloody arm. Hrym stands above you. He lifts the axe blade above his head and presses his foot on your chest.

"Hold still," he growls, before swinging his axe down and ending your life.

THE END

To follow another path, turn to page 11.
To learn more about Ragnarök, turn to page 101.

"My son," Odin says as you ride next to him. "I am glad you are with me. The enemy I face will be fierce."

His words worry you. Never before have you heard your father, the king of the gods, speak in fear.

Together you ride to the edge of the mountains. When you stop, you see the trees before you shake and crack. Tall pines fall over like sticks. You hear the heavy breathing of a giant creature pushing through the forest.

Moments later, the wolf Fenrir steps out from the woods. The ragged fur on his back reaches to the treetops. He growls and bares his fangs. They're like rows of swords. With each breath, fire flames from the beast's nostrils.

Odin climbs down from Sleipnir. You also start to climb down, but Odin holds up a hand.

"No. Stay here," he says.

The king of the gods strides forward, holding the spear Gungnir in both hands. Suddenly, the wolf leaps with his powerful jaws wide open. But Odin stands firm. He plunges his spear into the wolf's mouth.

Fenrir darts back, yelping in pain. The wolf shakes his head like a wet dog. The spear breaks free and flies from his mouth.

Fenrir lowers his head and glares at Odin. He snarls and digs his claws into the snowy ground. Then Fenrir lunges and snatches up Odin in his jaws. With one gulp, the wolf swallows him down.

You sit atop your horse, shocked and unable to move. Odin the wise, the king of the gods, the All-father, is gone—devoured by the great beast.

Turn the page.

Fenrir the wolf stands before you, baring its fangs. You pull out your sword and get ready to fight. But on the ground nearby you see Odin's spear, Gungnir. The spear's magic blade was forged by the dwarves. Its shaft is made of wood from Yggdrasil, the World Tree. You know that the spear never misses its mark.

To fight Fenrir with your sword, go to page 87.

To pick up Odin's spear, turn to page 91.

You pull out your sword and spur your horse toward Fenrir. You must use speed and surprise. The wolf looks confused at first. Then he looks hungry. He lowers his mouth to the ground and prepares to snatch you up in his jaws.

Suddenly, you stop the horse and leap at the wolf's throat. Fenrir snaps after the horse. You hold tightly to the wolf's mangy fur and try to plunge your sword into the beast.

But the sword's point can't pierce Fenrir's skin. You try to slash the monster with your weapon. But Fenrir's hide is like armor. The blade does not cut.

Fenrir shakes his head and sends you flying. You land on the snowy ground some distance away. The wolf turns and stalks toward you.

Your sword can't damage the wolf, and Odin's spear is too far away. What are you going to do?

Turn the page.

Fenrir was said to stand at least as tall as the trees of the forest. He could swallow the gods whole.

Then you remember. For years, you gathered strips of leather from the humans and wove them into your boots. You didn't know why you did this, but you knew there would be a reason one day. Now you know.

As you stand before Fenrir, the wolf opens his mouth to swallow you whole. But as his jaws come close, you stomp down on his tongue. Your special boots hold the wolf's jaw to the ground. Fenrir is stunned. He cannot move.

You plunge your sword through Fenrir's open mouth and into his throat. Then you leap out of the wolf's mouth. Fenrir chokes and gasps, and then falls over on its side. The great wolf is dead.

You look back across the plain of Vigrid. The battlefield is covered with bodies. You see Thor and his last enemy, the serpent. They both lie dead. Heimdall lies near Loki. They have killed each other in battle.

Loki's army, the frost giants, the Einherjar, the warriors of Muspell, the gods of Asgard—all are dead and lie scattered across the snowy plain.

Turn the page.

But there is one enemy who still walks. It is Surt the giant. You see him in the distance, with his flaming sword.

You also see two more figures on the battlefield. You narrow your eyes against the wind. It is Magni and Modi, Thor's sons. They carry Mjölnir, Thor's hammer, and are moving to face Surt.

Just then you notice something. You turn to see a ray of sunshine gleaming through bright green leaves. It is Yggdrasil, the World Tree. Perhaps the tree holds some secret that can help.

To fight Surt with the sons of Thor, turn to page 93.

To return to the World Tree, turn to page 95.

You leap from your horse and pick up Odin's spear. The weapon's weight balances perfectly in your hand. Fenrir watches you closely, looking for a chance to pounce.

Turn the page.

Odin's spear, Gungnir, was made by the dwarves. Its magical blade was said to never miss its target.

You slap the horse's flank and send it running. Fenrir watches the animal run off. As the wolf is distracted, you throw the spear.

Gungnir never misses its mark. The spear hits the wolf's throat. But even its magical blade can't pierce Fenrir's thick hide. The spear falls to the ground. The wolf turns and glares at you with a terrifying growl.

If Odin's magical spear can't pierce the wolf's hide, you know your sword won't either.

What am I going to do? you wonder.

But you don't have time to come up with a plan. Before you can act, Fenrir snaps you up in his mighty jaws. As all goes dark, you learn that your fate will be the same as your father's—in the wolf's belly.

THE END

To follow another path, turn to page 11.
To learn more about Ragnarök, turn to page 101.

When you catch up to Thor's sons, Magni speaks to you seriously. "We are the last of the gods. We must avenge those who have fallen."

Surt approaches in the distance. Together, Modi and Magni raise the hammer of Thor and prepare to fight.

The giant stops and laughs. "I do not fear your hammer. But you must fear my sword. It will bring an end to all the worlds."

The giant lifts his flaming sword over his head and swings it before himself. A wave of fire pours from the blade. You see the snow melt and the ground blacken before you. Surt swings the sword again, and an even larger wave of fire flows from the blade.

The flames pour in all directions. You see dead warriors, gods, and giants burn up like dried leaves in the intense heat.

Turn the page.

"Run!" shouts Magni. There is no choice. You must race to escape the flames.

Modi and Magni stop when you reach a rock ledge rising from the plain. They slam Mjölnir into the rock, and it splits. They swing the hammer again, and the rock crumbles before them. In front of you, a cave opens in the stone. It's wide and deep enough for the three of you to fit inside.

You climb into the opening just as the fire reaches you. The flames roar past the narrow cave. The fire's heat is like a hundred furnaces. But you are safe.

Turn to page 97.

You decide to investigate the World Tree. When you get there, you see you made it just in time. Looking back, you see flames pouring out from Surt's sword. A great fire floods across the plain of Vigrid in all directions.

You watch the flames burn up the lifeless bodies of warriors, gods, and giants on the battlefield. You also see Magni and Modi running from Surt, but the flames seem to quickly surround them.

Turn the page.

You climb Yggdrasil and take shelter in the giant tree's branches. The fire sweeps by like a strong wind. The heat is unlike anything you have felt before, yet the tree does not burn. You are safe among its branches. You wait for several days as the fire rages around you. Finally, the fire burns itself out.

When you look down to the plain of Vigrid, you see that the bodies of the fallen warriors, gods, giants, and monsters are gone. Even Surt is gone. The sun is shining. The snow has melted away. And the grass is growing.

You are surprised to hear voices—familiar voices. In the distance, you see Magni and Modi. Somehow, they survived the fire! You rush off to join them.

Later, as you and Thor's sons travel, you see that Surt's fire burned everything. All is gone, including the gods and humans, the giants and dwarves, and all of the nine worlds.

But you three have survived. You can feel the sun on your faces, and the grass is soft beneath your boots. Perhaps there is reason to have hope.

A short time later, you see a man and woman coming out from under Yggdrasil's roots. They brush off the dirt and laugh. Their names are Lif and Lifthrasir. They will build a house and raise a family. They will bring life back to the world.

Then you see another figure approaching. It is Baldur, beloved son of Odin, younger brother of Thor. Baldur has been in the Underworld for years after he was killed by Loki's trickery. Now he is free. You greet him with an embrace.

Turn the page.

The myth of Ragnarök says that a new world will emerge after Surt's fire wipes away the old age of the gods.

"Look what I found!" says Magni. He picks up something from the grass—a chess piece. You all get on your knees and find other pieces. They're in the shape of Odin, Thor, Frey, and all the gods.

"Here is Loki," you say. "And Surt and Hrym."

"And here is a board," says Modi. "Let's play."

"We should name this day," says Magni. "Let us call it Odin's Day."

"And we'll name the next day for Thor," you say.

You sit with the other gods in the green grass and enjoy the new life that has sprung up in the world. Together, you arrange the pieces and start a game. It is the dawning of a new age.

THE END

To follow another path, turn to page 11.
To learn more about Ragnarök, turn to page 101.

The Anglo-Saxon people began invading and settling in Britain in about 410 CE.

Chapter 5
A New Beginning

Today, we still have days named for Odin and Thor. Thor's Day is easy to spot. That's Thursday. But what about Odin's Day? Where is that on the calendar?

About 1,600 years ago, the island of Britain was invaded by the Anglo-Saxon people who worshipped the Norse gods. The language they spoke became the foundation of English, the language many people speak today. But English has changed a lot over the centuries.

The Anglo-Saxons called Odin by the name Woden. One of their days was called Wodensdag, or Woden's Day. Over time, that word changed to what we call Wednesday.

It's helpful to think of the days of the week when we try to understand the story of Ragnarök. Nearly all of the Norse gods die, along with all the giants, dwarves, monsters, humans, and animals. The nine worlds are then burned up by Surt's fire.

The gods and creatures of Norse mythology will all fight one another and meet their end at the final battle of Ragnarök.

Only a few gods survive, including Odin's son Vidar, Thor's sons Magni and Modi, and the god Baldur, who comes back from the Underworld. Two humans also survive: a woman named Lif and a man named Lifthrasir.

Why did the ancient people of northern Europe believe in a story where the world gets burned up and almost everyone dies?

Think of the days of the week. Although they are on a line across the calendar, they move like a circle. Many people go to work or school from Monday through Friday, and then there is the weekend. Then it all starts over again on Monday.

The ancient people who believed in the Norse gods thought of their lives like a circle. The circle of seasons told them when to plant crops, hunt for animals, or catch fish. They prepared for winter each year when crops didn't grow. And when spring came, they would plant food again.

Ragnarök was also believed to be part of a regular cycle. After everything is burned up by Surt's fire, the sun would come out, and the grass would grow once again.

Later, the gods who survive play a game with chess pieces that look like the old gods who died. The pieces represented the stories of the old gods, and they would last in people's memories.

Lif and Lifthrasir would be the start of new life for people in the world. The name Lif means "life," and Lifthrasir means "someone who loves life."

Ragnarök isn't just a story about the end of the world. Just as spring is the start of a new growing season and Monday is the start of a new week, Ragnarök is a story about the beginning of a whole new world.

Norse Family Tree

The ancient peoples of northern Europe believed in many gods. The gods were powerful beings, but they didn't live forever. The story of Ragnarök tells the story of how the most important gods and creatures in Norse mythology meet their doom.

YMIR

Many ancient Norse myths feature various giants. Ymir, the first being to appear in Norse mythology, was a giant of enormous size. The race of giants came from his body. The giants and the gods were often enemies in many stories.

THE GIANTS

SURT

a giant from the fiery world of Muspell. At Ragnarök, Surt's role is to bring fire and destroy the Norse cosmos to allow for the birth of a new world.

LOKI

Loki wasn't a god, but a giant. He often played tricks on the gods. But one of his tricks led to the death of Baldur, who was one of the most loved of all the gods. This event eventually led to Ragnarök.

LOKI + ANGRBODA

a giantess and mother to Loki's children

HEL

daughter of Loki and the ruler of the Underworld

SLEIPNIR

offspring of Loki, an eight-legged horse and the steed of Odin

JORMUNGAND

Often called the World Serpent, he was so large he could wrap around the entire world to bite his own tail. Jormungand's mortal enemy was Thor, and they were fated to kill one another at the final battle of Ragnarök.

FENRIR

a giant wolf and the offspring of Loki. Fenrir was fated to kill Odin, but then be killed by the god Vidar at Ragnarök.

THE GODS

BOR + BESTLA   a giantess

VILI   VE
brothers of Odin

ODIN
the All-father, the creator of the nine worlds, father to many gods, and the god of wisdom, battle, and poetry. If warriors lived good lives and died heroically, they would go to feast forever with Odin in his great hall called Valhalla.

ODIN + FRIGG   ODIN + EARTH   ODIN + GRID

THOR + SIF   wife of Thor
Thor was the most important of Odin's children and the strongest of the gods. In most of the ancient stories, Thor is shown killing giants. The ancient peoples of northern Europe believed that Thor protected them from many dangers.

VIDAR
a son of Odin, he was the god fated to kill the great wolf Fenrir. He wore a magical shoe that helped him hold open the wolf's huge jaws. He then killed the beast with his sword.

BALDUR
son of Odin and beloved by all the Norse gods

HEIMDALL
the watcher and guardian of the gods. His role was to guard the Rainbow Bridge that connected Asgard and Midgard. Heimdall was gifted in sight and could see far across the nine realms. He could even see into the future.

TYR   NJORD
sons of Odin

Other Paths to Explore

▶▶▶ Ancient peoples used myths to explain destructive natural events. Before people had knowledge of weather systems, they believed that natural disasters like earthquakes or hurricanes were caused by the gods or other mythical beings. What destructive part of nature does Surt the giant cause?

▶▶▶ Ancient peoples had to farm and hunt for their food. They paid attention to the changing seasons to know when to plant crops or hunt for game. In what ways is the story of Ragnarök similar to the changing seasons? If you were one of the gods who survived, what would be your role? How would you help the surviving people to thrive in the renewed world?

▶▶▶ The ancient Norse people told many stories of Thor and Odin. The enemies of these powerful figures were giants, monsters, and dead warriors. Today people enjoy many stories about superheroes, aliens, and zombies. How are our stories similar to the stories told by the ancient Norse people?

Bibliography

Crossley-Holland, Kevin. *The Norse Myths*. New York: Pantheon Books, 1980.

Gaiman, Neil. *Norse Mythology*. New York: W. W. Norton & Company, 2017.

Lindow, John. *Handbook of Norse Mythology*. Santa Barbara, CA: ABC-CLIO, 2001.

Norse Mythology for Smart People. https://norse-mythology.org/

Glossary

chain mail (CHAYN MAYL)—a kind of armor made from many iron rings linked together

forge (FORJ)—to form something by heating and hammering

mortal blow (MOHR-tuhl BLOW)—a strike or hit that causes someone to die

realm (RELM)—a region, such as a kingdom or a separate world, that belongs to a person or group

trickster (TRIK-ster)—a clever character in many folktales who often cheats or deceives others

tunic (TOO-nik)—an outer garment that covers the body and upper legs, usually worn with a belt

Underworld (UHN-duhr-wuhrld)—in ancient myths, the place where people went after death

Valhalla (vahl-HAH-luh)—in Norse mythology, the hall of Odin where the souls of heroes slain in battle go after death

Valkyrie (vahl-KEER-ee)—in Norse mythology, female helpers who bring slain warriors from the battlefield to Valhalla

vengeance (VEN-juhns)—something done to harm another person in return for an injury or damage done by that person

Read More

Bowen, Carl. *Gods and Thunder: A Graphic Novel of Old Norse Myths.* North Mankato, MN: Capstone Young Readers, 2017.

Kammer, Gina. *Can You Create the Norse Cosmos?: An Interactive Mythological Adventure.* North Mankato, MN: Capstone, 2023.

Nordvig, Mathias. *Norse Mythology for Kids: Tales of Gods, Creatures, and Quests.* Emeryville, CA: Rockridge Press, 2020.

Ralphs, Matt. *Norse Myths.* New York: DK, 2021.

Internet Sites

Children of Odin: Norse Mythology and Viking Legends
dltk-kids.com/world/norway/children-of-odin/index.htm

Kiddle: List of Norse Gods and Goddesses
kids.kiddle.co/List_of_Norse_gods_and_goddesses

The Vikings Gods and Myths
vikings.mrdonn.org/gods.html

About the Author

Bruce Berglund is a writer and historian. For two decades, he taught world history courses to college students. He has traveled in Europe, Asia, and South America. When he visited Iceland, he learned that Thor is a popular name there. Bruce grew up in Duluth, Minnesota, so he knows what it's like to live through the Mighty Winter.